Spank!

The Art of Fernando Caretta

Telling a story with a single illustrated image is very different from describing a simple erotic situation, because it's more static and the message is simply a sexual one. Closing an entire story in a single image, made of situations, elements and characters, means taking care of the expression of every character, their body language, gestures, every small detail...

I tend to stay on my pencils and manage my characters up to the point of exasperation, sometimes even having to redo almost completed illustrations.

I use coloured pencils, with cold and warm tones, to give a greater illusion of depth and when the piece is almost finished I use those same pencils to underline the important details.

When colouring I prefer pastel colours and a water-colour technique and on the base of that, I work with pantones and coloured pencils... The use of acrylic colours often completes the picture.
I also use other materials when colouring...

They may be rough or banal, but I can't reveal all my secrets...

Caretta

Spank! The Art of Fernando Caretta

Book design by Grassy Knoll Studios.

Published by SQP Inc. - PO Box 248 - Columbus NJ 08022

Sal Quartuccio & Bob Keenan - Publishers

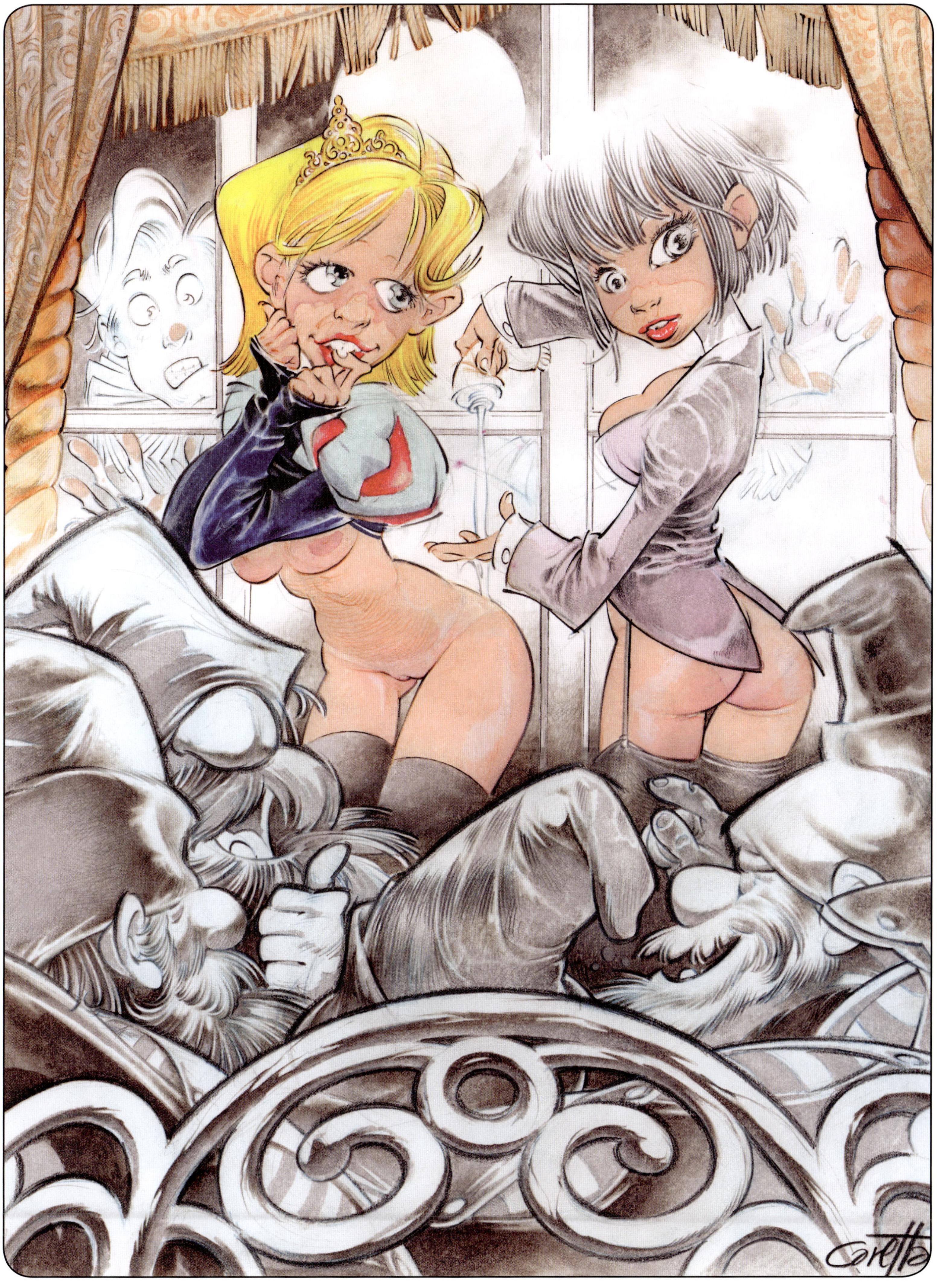

Caretta-

Caretta

Caretta

Caretta

MARY FUCK
W PUSSY
WC CULO
€5,00
€10,00
€20,00

Sex

Caretta

EXIT

TNT

TICKET
TICKET

Snow White
and the 7 Dwarfs

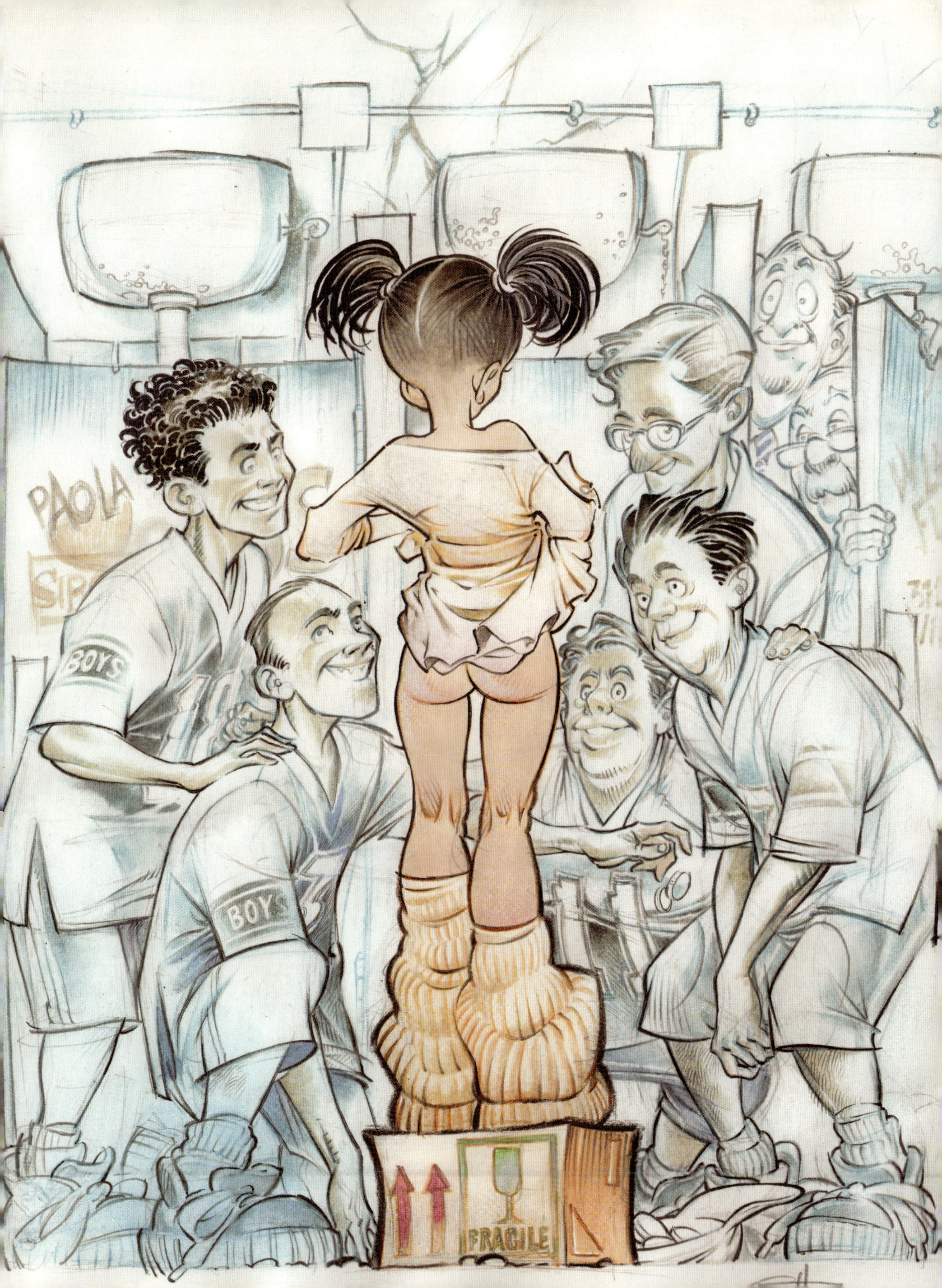
PAOLA
BOYS
BOYS
FRAGILE

Caretta-

Coretta-

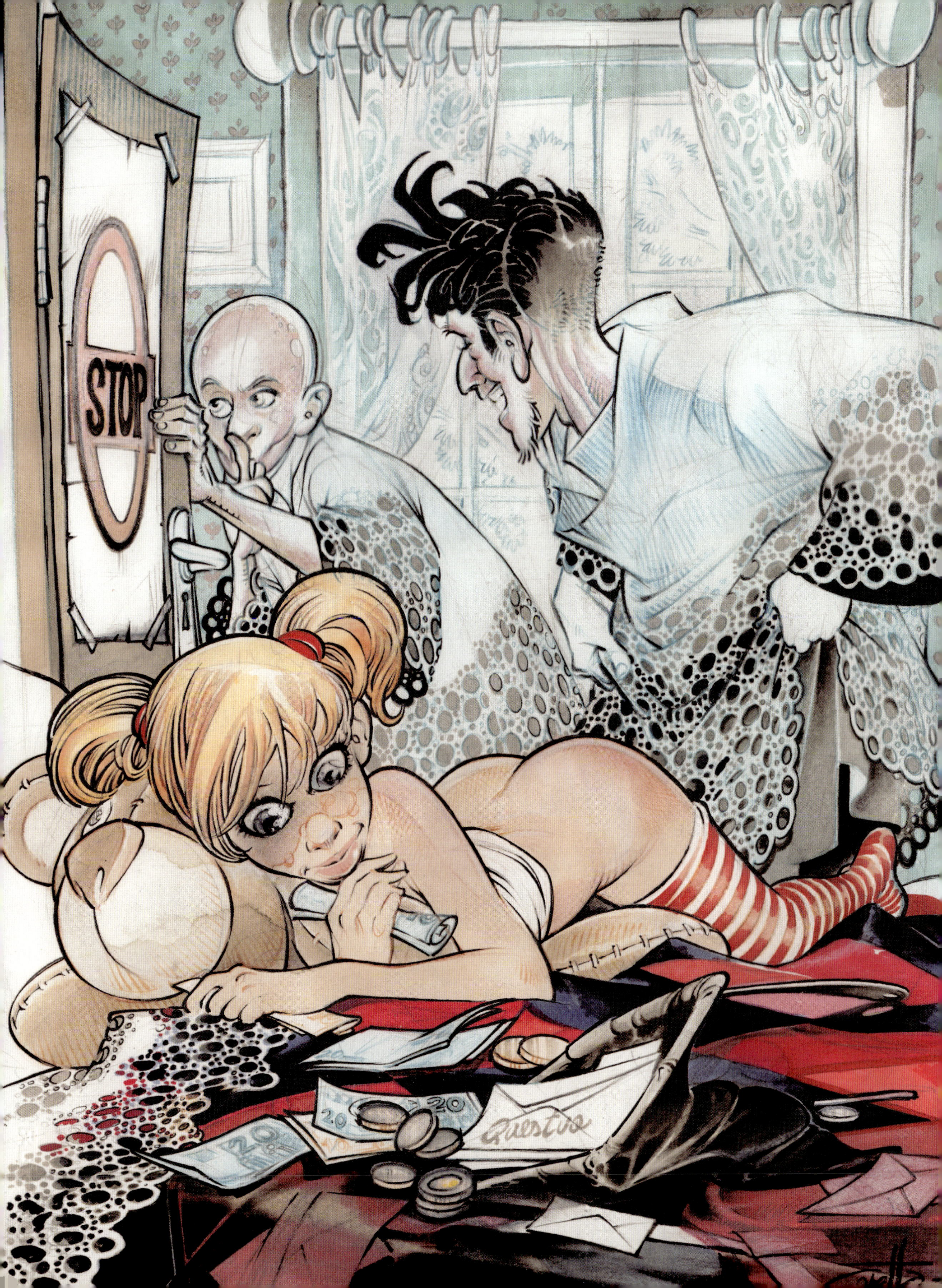
STOP

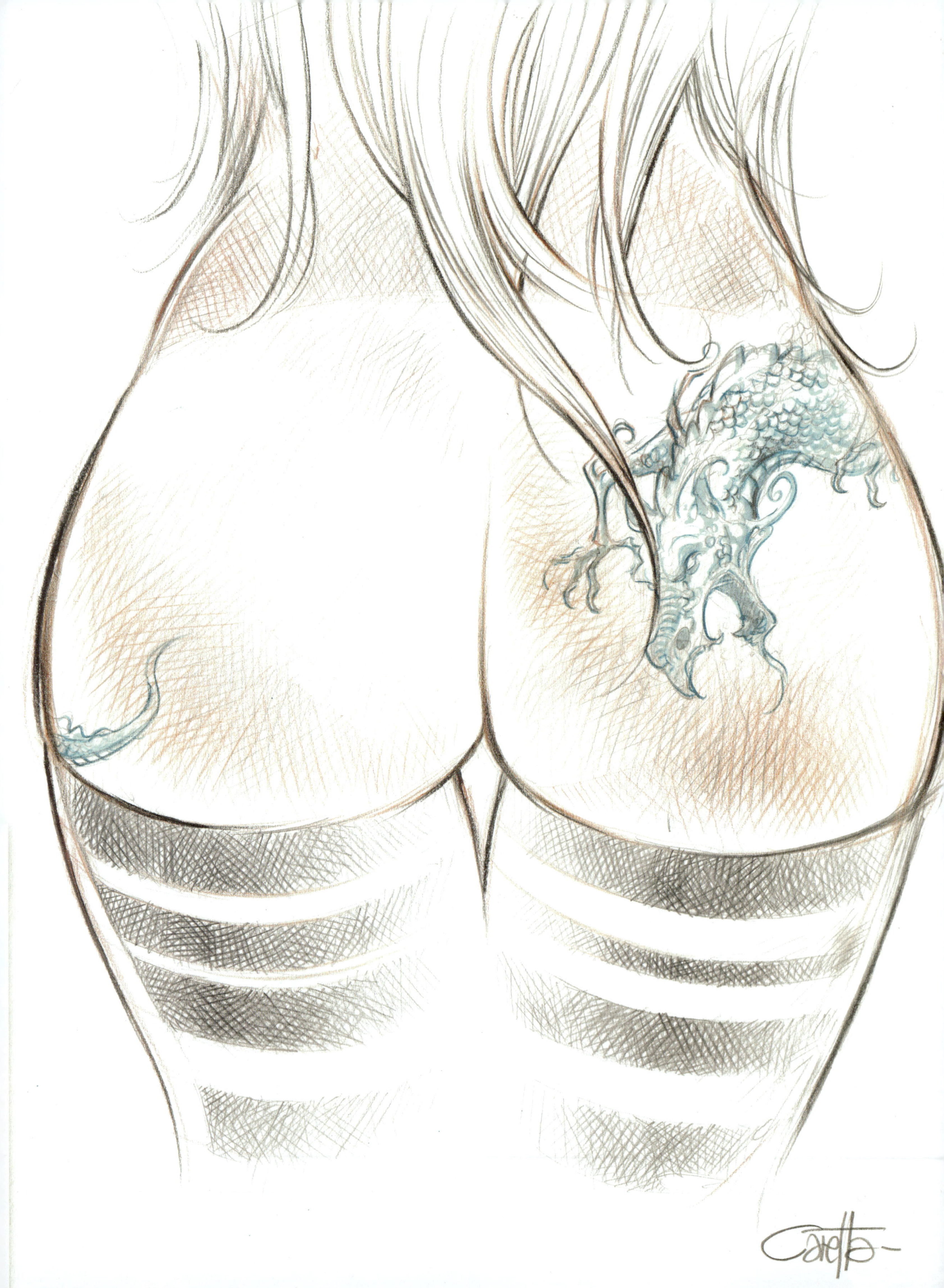

Caretta-

SUPERHEROINE